W9-ARB-521

NO ACTUAL ISSUES OF RIGHT AND WRONG
ARE SOLVED IN THIS BOOK.

KNOWING RIGHT FROM WRONG MAY COME FROM INSIDE,
OR YOU MAY LEARN IT, BUT IF YOU REALLY THINK YOU CAN GET
IT FROM A BUNNY, IT MAY ALREADY BE TOO LATE FOR YOU.

FOR THE SAKE OF MANKIND, PLEASE DO NOT LEARN
THIS SORT OF THING FROM BUNNIES.

it's happy bunny™

The Good, the Bad, and the Bunny

By Jim Benton

SCHOLASTIC INC.

New York Toronto London Auckland Sydney
Mexico City New Delhi Hong Kong Buenos Aires
Wheretheheckistan

For Beth, Bob, Carole, Jodi,
Ken, Lauren, Liz, and Ria

Bipolar thanks to Maria Barbo, Craig Walker, Shannon Penney, Steve Scott, Susan Jeffers Casel, Kara Edwards and Kay Petronio, who may be bad, but are good at what they do.

ISBN 13: 978-0-439-70593-6

ISBN 10: 0-439-70593-2

Copyright ©2006 by Jim Benton

12 11 10 9 8 7 6 5 4 3 2 1   6 7 8 9 10 11/0

Printed in Mexico

First printing, November 2006

Published by Scholastic against all better judgment.

Maybe you know who you are.

You might even know
where you are.

But do you know
what you are?

In this book, we'll examine the difference between good and bad through examples, quizzes, games, and bits of bunny wisdom which, like pimples, will suddenly appear for no reason, and then just dry up and go away.

These will be helpfully labeled: Bunny Wisdom.

Good or bad. Is it always that simple? Let's start with a quiz. Look deep within yourself for the answers.

(If I catch you looking deep within the people sitting next to you, you will have to retake this quiz after school.)

Quiz Time!

Do you know the difference
between right and wrong?
A. Yes.   B. No.

Answer: If you did know, you wouldn't have
tried to read the answer upside down before
you answered the question, like the big cheater
you are.

Since you don't know the difference, maybe we can at least pretend that you do.

Because faking it is a great way to show that you care enough to lie.

Chapter One
Opening the Door to Your Inner Goodness

(Your creamy goodness.)

Have a look at this example:
Let's say you hold a door
open for somebody and they
walk through without saying
thank you.

The Good Thing To Do: Don't worry about it. You didn't hold the door open to get a thank you. That would be selfish.

The Bad Thing To Do:
Slam their head in the door over and over and over and over.

The Bunny Thing To Do:
Tell them you saw them drop
some money outside. When
they go back out to find it,
lock the door.

I know what you're thinking:

Are you
SURE it's not the
slamming one?

Okay, the slamming one
is pretty good.

20228548

Nobody is perfect.

And by "nobody,"
of course I mean
"nobody else."

Here's another example:
Let's say you lend somebody
your favorite DVD and they
lose it.

The Good Thing To Do:
Forgive them. If it was that
precious to you, you should
not have lent it.

The Bad Thing To Do:
Borrow one of their DVDs.
Explain later that you accidentally
tried to play it in the toaster.

The Bunny Thing To Do:
Lend this loser the things that
you want to lose, but don't want
to get blamed for losing: math
book, ugly hat from Grandma,
your little brother, etc.

I know what you're thinking again:

I spent too much for this book.

Maybe you did, and that could
have been a bad thing, except
that it worked out in my favor,
so I'm going to have to call
that a good thing.
See? It's complicated.

Never insult somebody holding dog poop and a tennis racket.

Another example of the
Bunny Thing To Do:
Let's say you know a person
who is always stinky. Maybe
it's bad breath, maybe they're
afraid of baths. Whatever.

The Good Thing To Do:
Get over it. People can
smell however they want
to. Nobody made you the
President of Armpits.

The Bad Thing To Do:
Give them a pair of air
fresheners as a gift and tell
them that they're earrings.

The Bunny Thing To Do:

Why do anything? Now you have the perfect place to go when you have to fart. While you're standing next to them, who would ever blame you?

You can never
know a person until
you've walked a
mile in their shoes.

**And you probably never
will know them, because
they're, like, a mile
behind you and now
they're barefoot.**

Are you starting to understand
yet? Here's another one:
Let's say your mean aunt gets
a new dress and asks you,
"Do I look fat in this?"

The Good Thing To Say:
"Are you kidding? You look
like a million bucks."

The Bad Thing To Say:
"Why don't the three of you
come out of that tent and
we'll talk about it."

The Bunny Thing To Say:
"Don't be silly."

And here's why this works . . .

. . . She'll think you mean "Don't be silly. You look perfect." Even though what you really mean is, "Don't be silly. Of course you look fat. How else could you look?"

So I didn't lie, which would be wrong, and I didn't hurt my aunt's feelings, which would also be wrong.

You see the point? Good and bad can be *relative* terms.

I'll bet that means that no matter how good you are to your relatives, they'll still say bad things about you.

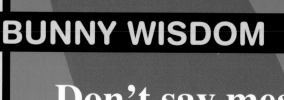

BUNNY WISDOM

Don't say mean
things to people.

Until they
put down the
garden hose.

QUIZ TIME!

Stealing is wrong, but if you're starving to death, is it okay to steal a potato?
A. Yes.
B. No.

See? Sometimes it isn't
so easy to know the difference
between good and bad.

But I know choking
on a potato is bad.

BUNNY WISDOM

You can lead a horse to water, but you can't make him drink.

But you can make
him drown. And when
you remind him of
that, he'll probably be
willing to drink.

Chapter Two
The Useful Fable

Let's try one of those fables that are so useful for teaching lessons about good and bad.

(Don't worry, there won't be a quiz on this.)

Once there were these two
people who really liked each
other. But they were very poor.

All she had was beautiful
long hair and all he had was a
magnificent pocket watch.

She decided to sell her hair
to the wig maker and use the
money to buy him a chain
for his watch.

"I bet I know why," she said.
"I bet it was so that you could
buy me a comb for my hair."

He looked at her and smiled.
"Wrong-o," he said.

"I used the money to buy several pies, which I ate. Your hair looks dumb that way. You should change it back."

Weeks later, he learned that she was dating the wig maker.

Moral

Sometimes doing the wrong
thing might get you pie, but
that's all it will get you.

And, sometimes doing
the right thing will get
you even less.

———

SURPRISE QUIZ!
on the USEFUL FABLE

Since reading the Useful Fable, I feel that it is wrong to:

A. Selfishly disregard the feelings of the people that care about me.

B. Witlessly assume that everybody I know is going to do the right thing just because I do.

C. Pay too much for pie.

D. Assume people are telling me the truth when they say there won't be a quiz.

Answer: C. But now it occurs to me that you can also pay too much for a book.

Chapter Three
Fun and Games

(You have nothing to
lose but your soul.)

How Not to Speak Your Mind

There is a GOOD WAY and a BAD WAY to say almost everything. And, luckily, there's also a BUNNY WAY.

Read on and determine how you want to say things.

The GOOD WAY to say it: "Casual"

The BAD WAY to say it: "Sloppy"

The BUNNY WAY to say it:
"Pro-Bacterial"

The GOOD WAY to say it: "Senior"

The BAD WAY to say it: "Old"

The BUNNY WAY to say it:
"High belter"

The GOOD WAY to say it: "Big"

The BAD WAY to say it: "Fat"

The BUNNY WAY to say it:
"Salad intolerant"

The GOOD WAY to say it: "Thinning"

The BAD WAY to say it: "Bald"

The BUNNY WAY to say it:
"Gentle on the combs"

The GOOD WAY to say it: "Plain"

The BAD WAY to say it: "Ugly"

The BUNNY WAY to say it:
"Nice-looking in a non-facey kind of way"

The GOOD WAY to say it: "Naive"

The BAD WAY to say it: "Stupid"

The BUNNY WAY to say it:
"Lifelong finger painter"

Hey, I know —
let's try a real-life example.

(Just make your choices and follow the arrows.)

Let's say you find a bag of money.
What do you do with it?

KEEP IT.

TURN IT IN TO THE POLICE.

JUST LEAVE IT THERE.

Eventually, somebody will find out you did this.

Okay, I'm nervous. I guess I'll . . .

You sure? Nobody is making you turn it in.

Just leave it there? REALLY?

YEAH. Here's my plan. . . .

I'm still keeping it.

THEN I'LL KEEP IT.

I'm still DOING it.

THAT'S THE SAME AS STEALING AND YOU'LL GO TO JAIL FOR FIVE YEARS.

THE POLICE WILL ASSUME YOU'RE CRAZY AND HAVE YOU LOCKED UP FOR SIX YEARS.

SOMEBODY ELSE WILL FIND IT. IN A WEEK, I'LL CALL THE POLICE AND TELL THEM I LOST IT. THEN THEY'LL JUST GIVE IT TO ME.

Except that it's still stealing. And lying.

It IS clever, isn't it?

And GUESS WHAT? Police read this book, too, and now they're on to your scheme. You'll get ten years for this, for sure.

Hey, that's pretty clever.

The only truly safe thing to do is to never find a big bag of money in the first place, so try not to do that as often as possible.

However, if you are ever unfortunate enough to find one, just send it here and we'll take care of it for you.

**IT'S HAPPY BUNNY
P.O. BOX 1354
Birmingham, MI 48012**

My Life
Pledge

Just choose the words that best suit how you feel.

This pledge will be the one that you must live by for the rest of your life, so please take a couple of minutes to think over your answers.

I, (your name), promise that I will always try to do my
best second best dishes. And in those instances where I
make a mistake, I will go back and try to make it right better
look like somebody else did it. Because I know that in the end,
I will be judged by the things I say do neglect to conceal.

I will always remember that others are also doing their
best second best laundry, and although we won't always
agree on the difference between good and bad (because
everybody is different stupid a totally huge stupidhead), at
least we can agree that people are basically good bad beasts,
and if you keep that in mind you will never be disappointed
lend one money permit them on your furniture.

I hope that I will never lose my sense of justice smell
fashion, but if I do, I'm sure I can count on my friends and
family to help me recover it eat my pie over a cliff, because
that is exactly what I would do for them.

_____

(sign your name)
(or forge somebody else's name who you think should take this pledge)

Remember that there are two sides to everything.

Your side and the wrong one.

Congratulations!

Now you're an expert on good and bad. All that's left is to keep track of the good and bad things in the world, so you know when to brag and when to blame somebody else.

THE GOOD THINGS I'VE DONE:

_____
_____
_____
_____
_____
_____
_____
_____
_____
_____
_____
_____
_____
_____
_____
_____
_____
_____

THE BAD THINGS I'VE DONE:

_____
_____

THE BAD THINGS MY FRIENDS AND FAMILY HAVE DONE:

_____
_____
_____
_____
_____
_____
_____
_____
_____
_____
_____
_____
_____
_____
_____
_____
_____

THE GOOD THINGS THEY'VE DONE:

_____
_____

We should all
be nice.

**Even the stupid
ugly people.**